JOSEPH CHAMBERLAIN'S HIGHBURY: A VERY PUBLIC PRIVATE HOUSE

Stephen Roberts

Published under the imprint *Birmingham Biographies*

Printed by CreateSpace

© Stephen Roberts, 2015

All rights reserved. No part of this publication may be reproduced in any form, stored in or re-introduced into a retrieval system, or transmitted, in any form or by any means, electronic, mechanical, photocopying, recording or otherwise without the prior consent of the author.

The moral right of Stephen Roberts to be identified as the author of this work has been asserted in accordance with the Copyright, Designs and Patents Act 1988.

ISBN-13: 978-1515044680

ISBN-10: 1515044688

Front cover: A range of postcards of Joseph Chamberlain's very public private house, including this colour one, could be bought during his lifetime.

To the memory of my grandfather Reg Williams (1902-1981), who worked in the gardens of Sir George Kenrick.

Contents

Contents i

Acknowledgements ii

Preface iv

Joseph Chamberlain's Highbury: A Very Public Private House 1

Illustrations 17

About the Author 36

Acknowledgements

This pamphlet evolved from an after-dinner talk I gave at Highbury in July 2014 to mark the centenary of the death of Joseph Chamberlain. Several months before the dinner, I spent a morning wandering from room-to-room in an empty Highbury and I am very grateful to the staff employed by Birmingham City Council who gave me permission to do this.

The Cadbury Research Library in the University of Birmingham is an extremely congenial place in which to work. I wish to thank the staff who brought out material for me faster than I could sharpen my pencil, and who also responded helpfully to all my queries by email. The staff of the Wolfson Centre for Archival Research in the Library of Birmingham, another very pleasant place to work, have also been of great assistance

I am most grateful to Kathryn Rix for her encouraging comments about this essay and for picking up a number of slips during the close reading she gave it. I also benefitted from a useful conversation with Philidda Ballard about the gardens at Highbury.

I am indebted to Peter James and the Library of Birmingham for permission to reproduce a number of the photographs.

Thanks also to Richard Brown for his technical expertise.

I dedicate this essay to the memory of my grandfather Reg Williams (1902-1981), who worked at one time in the orchid houses of Sir George Kenrick at Whetstone, Somerset Road, Edgbaston. My grandfather remembered often seeing Neville Chamberlain visiting the orchid houses at his uncle's house.

Joseph Chamberlain in one of his orchid houses at Highbury, 1902.

Preface

During the second half of the nineteenth century the country houses of leading statesmen became part of the political vocabulary. Gladstone's Hawarden, Disraeli's Hughenden, Salisbury's Hatfield House would all have been familiar place names to those who took an interest in politics. As a man with great ambitions for himself in the political world, and with a son who was being made ready to follow in his footsteps, Joseph Chamberlain wished to own a house that reflected his status and importance. The men who shaped Birmingham in this period were self-made industrialists and did not inherit grand homes built by distinguished ancestors, and so they set about building their own impressive houses, often employing the noted civic architect J.H. Chamberlain, who favoured the use of red brick decorated by terracotta. Highbury, situated several miles south of the town centre, became the Birmingham home of Joseph Chamberlain and his family in 1880. Joe's three oldest children were to live at Highbury and Prince's Gardens in London for much of their early adult lives; Austen, for example, lived in his father's houses until 1903 when, at the age of forty, he was appointed Chancellor of the Exchequer. The three younger daughters, aged between ten and seven, grew up at Highbury, which they greatly preferred to Prince's Gardens. But Highbury was more than a family home; it was also a public symbol, a physical reminder of Joe's national importance and local political control. Statesmen regularly arrived to be entertained and to formulate their political plans at Highbury, and were photographed on the terrace which overlooked the magnificent gardens, another feature designed to impress. The house and gardens were widely written about in the newspapers and magazines of the day. This essay, drawing on this material and personal recollections, offers a glimpse into life in a very public private house.

Joseph Chamberlain's Highbury: A Very Public Private House

When Joseph Chamberlain was returned unopposed as the third Member for Birmingham in summer 1876 - his colleagues were John Bright and Philip Muntz - he was living in Edgbaston, at Southbourne, a house he had had built for himself, in Augustus Road.[1] His closest allies, men like the ministers George Dawson and R.W. Dale and the newspaper editor J.T. Bunce, were regularly invited to dine at Southbourne and afterwards, over cigars in the library, talked about local politics and how they would transform their town. It was here, too, that Chamberlain developed his interest in horticulture, particularly the growing of orchids. But this house, impressive as it was with its panelled ceilings and carved oak fittings, did not match the scale of Chamberlain's ambitions. With his sights set on high office, if not the eventual leadership of his party, from the beginnings of his parliamentary career, Chamberlain needed something grander than a town house, somewhere that would unequivocally demonstrate his political status and influence.[2] So it was that, in early 1878, he bought twenty five acres of land in Moor Green in Moseley, four miles south of the centre of Birmingham, with the intention of building himself a country mansion. His younger brother the electric lighting manufacturer Arthur lived in the adjoining property Moor Green Hall, and Joe's children were always to refer to their relations as 'the Moor Greens'.

---

[1] S. Roberts and R. Ward *Mocking Men of Power: Comic Art in Birmingham 1861-1911* (Birmingham, 2014), pp. 22-5 for Bright and Muntz as Birmingham MPs.

[2] Bright stayed at Southbourne when he made his short visits to Birmingham, or alternatively at The Dales, the Edgbaston home of his fellow MP George Dixon. William Gladstone was a guest at Chamberlain's home when he came to Birmingham in May 1877 to launch the National Liberal Federation; another regular visitor was the Liberal editor and essayist John Morley. Southbourne was briefly the residence of the brewer Walter Showell, also a keen grower of orchids and other plants, 'many of which have taken valuable prizes at local shows' (*Birmingham Daily Post,* 20 October 1883).

I

'Mr Chamberlain is building a magnificent residence at Highbury, near Birmingham', it was reported in the provincial press in summer 1880. 'The new place, it is said, will match, if it does not eclipse, the seats of the neighbouring gentry'.[3] The architects who designed Chamberlain's new house, William Martin and J.H. Chamberlain – who was not a relation - of 53 Ann Street, left, in a different, but equally important, way, as much of a mark on their town as Joe himself did. Across Birmingham they sought to raise the standard of civic architecture with ornately-designed board schools, libraries, hospitals and fire stations. One architectural historian has aptly described their 'lively Ruskinian Gothic style ... (as being) the brand of the Civic Gospel'.[4] The plans of his architects must have impressed Chamberlain when he first perused them in summer 1878. There were 22 rooms on the ground floor of his new mansion, including an imposing hall 40' long and 30' wide, and, on the first floor, 12 bedrooms and three water closets. Martin and Chamberlain also thoughtfully included a huge safe and a lift for those who preferred to admire rather than climb the very fine staircase.[5]

Chamberlain's third daughter Hilda recalled that 'we used to drive over pretty often to see how the house was getting on. Papa was always very gay on these excursions, laughing and joking ... these were real red-letter days'.[6] However, the London journalists who were invited to visit Joe's red-tinted brick and white stone mansion in the ensuing years didn't find themselves in raptures about the sight that greeted them. For sure, they thought that on its south facing slope it was imposing enough, but hardly a sight of great beauty. Highbury was, one reporter wrote, 'by no means

---

[3] *Liverpool Echo*, 24 August 1880.
[4] J. Holyoak, 'J.H. Chamberlain' in P. Ballard ed. *Birmingham's Victorian and Edwardian Architects* (2009), pp. 153-81. For a useful discussion of the widespread use by late Victorian provincial architects of terracotta, see M. Stratton, 'William Watkins and the Terracotta Revival' in *The Victorian Façade: W. Watkins and Son, Architects, Lincoln, 1859-1918* (reptd. Lincoln, 2013), pp. 24-8.
[5] Library of Birmingham, MS133813, Architectural Plans for Highbury.
[6] University of Birmingham, Cadbury Research Library, BC5/10/6.

palatial ... it is simply a large, well-built, thoroughly pleasant and comfortable modern house'.[7]

Highbury, however, was built not to please the eye but to enhance the impression that a man of immense political importance was to be found inside it. It was fashionable for wealthy manufacturers to name their big houses after places with which they had once been personally associated – Uffculme, the Devon village where Richard Cadbury grew up, also became the name of the mansion he built near Highbury in 1891 – but, as Chamberlain's biographer has suggested, it was also a deliberate political calculation on his part to name his house after the London suburb where he spent his early years.[8] His impressive house also served, however, as a physical reminder that the political situation in Birmingham and its environs were very much under his control.

During parliamentary sessions Chamberlain lived at Highbury from only Saturday to Monday and during the recesses he was often fishing in Scotland or on the Continent – but the name of his mansion soon entered the political lexicon of late nineteenth century and early twentieth century Britain. Highbury garden parties were chosen for well-reported speeches on issues of the moment, statements flowed from his library, political colleagues came to stay, and newspapers reported when Chamberlain had arrived at, or left, his mansion. The house served as a political base for Chamberlain and, though his four daughters Beatrice, Ida, Hilda and Ethel lived there – Austen was at Cambridge and then abroad and Neville was at Rugby – and his brother Arthur occupied an adjacent house, it did not offer him the privacy that he enjoyed at 40 Prince's Gardens, the home he bought in London's West End in 1883.

---

[7] *Evening Telegraph*, 5 December 1902. The reporter was N. Murrell Marris, the author of a flattering biography of Chamberlain (1900).
[8] P. Marsh, *Joseph Chamberlain: Entrepreneur in Politics* (1994), p. 139: 'He called it Highbury ... In doing so he suggested that his seat should command attention from the perspective of London as well as Birmingham'.

II

Chamberlain was a man with two butlers – and indeed two of everything, apart from footmen, of which he had four. In total he employed about a dozen servants in each of his houses. The census returns for Highbury tell us the names, roles, ages and geographical origins of the servants. Let us look at 1891. The servants were, for the most part, in their twenties – the exceptions include Fred Down, the 58-year old odd job man, and Elizabeth Williams, the 39-year old cook. To prevent gossip about what was happening in the house, none of the servants had local connections. Thus, Harry Clack, the 26-year old butler and Annie Hardy, the 18-year old house maid, originated in Chipping Norton and Derby respectively. There were another three adults and two children living in the lodge and twenty gardeners who lived in the vicinity - in all Chamberlain was employing 34 adults at Highbury in 1891. When the family moved into Highbury, Chamberlain, a widower for the second time, left the employment of the servants and other domestic arrangements to his sister Clara – though it was to their father that his daughters looked to ensure there were more currants in the bread and butter pudding - but, for several years until his third marriage to Mary Endicott in 1888, this became the unwanted responsibility of his eldest daughter Beatrice.[9] At Christmas-time the servants were paid a bonus.

The butler Harry Clack was left red-faced when, on the evening of 6 April 1891, a burglary took place at Highbury. It was Clack's responsibility to ensure that, when the family were at home, all doors and windows were locked by seven o'clock in the evening. Clack neglected, however, to ensure that the front doors and a nearby lavatory window were locked, with the result that shortly after seven o'clock James Fitzgerald and two other men climbed in through the window and left by the front doors, taking with them five walking sticks decorated with silver and two riding whips. The three men swiftly sold the items they had purloined, but later that evening, in a public house, quarrelled during a game of cards. With his companion 'Big Dick' Short turning Queen's Evidence against

---

[9] University of Birmingham, Cadbury Research Library, BC5/10/5. Their request that they no longer be served tapioca, 'which we all loathed', was also conveyed by Chamberlain to his sister.

him, Fitzgerald faced the retribution of the authorities alone. His evening venture into the vestibule of Joe's house led to a prison sentence of five years in July 1891.[10]

Security at Highbury was in fact tight. There was a lodge at the entrance to the grounds, occupied in 1891 by 48-year old Edward Cooper and his family. Visitors stopped first at the lodge, and Cooper kept an eye out for potential intruders. There was in fact only one more attempt at entering the house. In June 1913, when Chamberlain and his wife were in Cannes, jemmy marks were found around the doors, but no entry took place. Though there was no credible evidence that the Fenians actually planned to blow up Highbury in summer 1886 after he made clear his opposition to Irish Home Rule, Chamberlain took the reports seriously enough to arrange for a police officer to remain in the house for several weeks.[11] The Fenians might not have appeared at Highbury, but, in January 1889, a con man, and in June 1902, the 'Son of God', certainly did. The con man was Ernest Rolte who passed himself off to Austen Chamberlain, with a forged letter of introduction, as one of his father's American friends. Rolte enjoyed a tour of the orchid houses and, pleading a lost wallet, duped Austen out of £10 before a few days later cashing a forged cheque at Austen's bank. He was last heard of in St. Albans, where, claiming to be Austen, he made away with a supply of orchids. The 'Son of God' - we don't know his actual name - was confronted by a police officer, at midnight on 2 June 1902. After 'a desperate struggle' he was 'conveyed ... to Kings Heath police station where he was certified as a dangerous lunatic and removed to the county asylum'.[12]

There were more welcome visitors to Highbury than fraudsters and fruitcakes. Chamberlain would regularly invite leading political figures to stay for two or three nights. John Bright enjoyed Chamberlain's hospitality when, at the beginning of each year, he made his customary visit to the town he represented. Sir Charles Dilke sought refuge at Highbury in August 1885 when he was

---

[10] *Western Gazette*, 10 April 1891; *Worcestershire Chronicle*, 2 May 1891; *Leeds Times*, 4 July 1891.

[11] *Manchester Courier*, 1 July 1886; *Worcester Journal*, 3 July 1886; *Aberdeen Journal*, 2 June 1913.

[12] *Western Times*, 31 January 1889; *Edinburgh Evening News*, 20 August 1889; *Evening Telegraph*, 4 June 1902.

accused of seducing a young married woman. It had been Dilke who had ushered Chamberlain into the London political scene after his election to Parliament, and Joe stood by his friend during this harrowing period, offering advice and agreeing to be his best man during his stay at Highbury. Chamberlain's longstanding friendship with John Morley was fractured by the Irish Home Rule crisis of 1886, but it was not a relationship he wanted to let go – in June 1889 Morley accepted an invitation to visit Highbury. The Unionist MPs Richard Mallock and James Rankin spent a weekend at Highbury in November 1891 poring over the details of an Old Age Pensions Bill. The Duke of Devonshire, the Whiggish Liberal who, in 1886, had worked with Chamberlain to bring down the Home Rule Bill, was a guest at Highbury in December 1895. The two men shared an interest in imperial defence, though it was always an uneasy relationship: Devonshire later refused to support the tariff reform campaign. Many other leading figures of the day – almost all of them politicians, for Chamberlain had no friendships outside politics – were invited to stay at Highbury. A local photographer, usually the highly-regarded John Collier of New Street, was employed to record many of these visits.[13]

Up until Chamberlain succumbed to a stroke in July 1906, there was a formal dinner with guests at Highbury each weekend – usually on the Saturday. The year would begin with a family dinner, but otherwise those attending were political colleagues. On occasions, if Chamberlain had special business with a colleague, only two or three would be present, but mostly these gatherings were quite large. On 25 January 1889 – a month in which there was the unusually high tally of eight dinners – 28 people sat down to dinner. The adjutant-general at the War Office Lord Wolseley and his wife, who were staying at Highbury for a few days, were amongst them and had the pleasure of meeting, amongst an impressive array

---

[13] University of Birmingham, Cadbury Research Library, C/4/11; *Grantham Journal,* 14 November 1881; *Leicester Chronicle,* 2 February 1884; *Portsmouth Evening News,* 10 January 1885; *Dundee Courier,* 1 August 1885; *Birmingham Daily Post,* 6 May 1889; *Yorkshire Evening Post,* 9 January 1899.

of local politicians, the mayor of Birmingham R.C. Barrow.[14] All the local movers and shakers could be found gathered around Chamberlain's dining table at some point in the year – the ministers R.W. Dale and Henry Crosskey, his old Liberal allies George Dixon and J. Powell Williams and his new-found Tory friends Frank Lowe and Sir Benjamin Stone. Jesse Collings had Chamberlain's ear more than most – in January 1889 he ate his dinner at Highbury on three occasions. These dinners weren't abandoned after Chamberlain became incapacitated, but they certainly fell away. Sir Edward Carson and Andrew Bonar Law joined his local political allies at his table on 21 November 1913. This wasn't intended to be Chamberlain's final big dinner at Highbury, but that is how it turned out.[15]

Those who arrived for the weekend or for dinner on a Saturday evening could not fail to be impressed by the opulence they encountered at Highbury. Beatrice Potter found the house oppressive and sombre – and the north side, including the dining room, was certainly dark – but other visitors greatly admired the marble pillars, the coloured tiles, the parquet floors, the ceilings inlaid with panels of shamrock and ivy, the huge fern in the middle of the hall, the ebony furniture decorated with ivory and the paintings which adorned every wall.[16] Though he had no interest in music – 'almost entirely tone deaf', the only tune he could identify with certainty was the National Anthem – Chamberlain was 'a great lover of pictures ... particularly delighting in the English watercolours';[17] there was a preponderance of highly detailed

---

[14] A Quaker grocer, with shops in Bull Street and Corporation Street, Barrow was a leading advocate of early closing. He died suddenly in October 1894.

[15] University of Birmingham, Cadbury Research Library, C/4/11, C/4/12. Also BC5/10/6 for Hilda's memories of dances in the hall at Highbury – 'neither Neville nor Austen were ... easily taken with girls' – and of weekend parties 'when the house was filled with interesting people from London or strangers over the summer from America or elsewhere'.

[16] N. and J. MacKenzie eds. *The Diary of Beatrice Webb* (1982), I, pp. 105-6.

[17] University of Birmingham, Cadbury Research Library, BC5/10/6. Hilda Chamberlain remembered her father regularly visiting art galleries during holidays on the continent, being especially impressed by the work of Diego Velazquez in Madrid in 1894.

watercolour landscapes at Highbury, works by the famous Copley Fielding – who produced paintings very quickly to meet high demand – and by Harborne resident David Cox – who turned out depictions of North Wales – and by A.W. Hunt. Chamberlain also liked classical and historical subjects, paying high prices for paintings by Frederick Leighton – who had the misfortune to die the day after he was awarded a peerage – and by Marcus Stone. There were, of course, also family portraits. Likenesses of Chamberlain's parents were displayed alongside the watercolours in the dining room. Chamberlain commissioned portraits of himself and his third wife Mary by the best men money could buy, John Singer Sargent and John Everett Millais. His own imposing portrait was presented to Mary on their wedding day in December 1888. The two portraits were put to good use, embellishing the staircase.

Once their desire to admire the landscapes had been sated, visitors could turn their attention to the vast array of curios that had found their way from various parts of the world to Highbury. These gifts increased significantly in number after Chamberlain's appointment as Colonial Secretary in 1895, and in January 1897 Austen began work on a catalogue. Amongst the items he recorded were spears, swords, a shield made of rhinoceros' hide, the very bandolier worn by Paul Kruger's son-in-law, a stuffed flamingo, paddles, musical instruments, medals, horns – 27 of them – and clocks – one made by a soldier wounded at Mafeking and another that once belonged to Queen Victoria. Joe was doubtless delighted to add to the head of a bison he had acquired in November 1878, the head of a large antelope in August 1896. 'Sent over with the entire animal (frozen) as a present ... from Sir James Sieve-Wright, Minister of the Cape Colony', Austen noted in his catalogue.[18]

III

How did Chamberlain spend his time when he was at Highbury? Certainly he avoided physical exertion. 'He does not ride, he does not play golf', one journalist observed. 'There is no billiard table in the house, he never walks more than he can help ...'[19] After eating breakfast with his family and looking through his post, Hilda

---

[18] University of Birmingham, Cadbury Research Library, AC1/7/1.
[19] *Weekly Scotsman,* 8 July 1899.

remembered her father 'striding across the big hall, with a newly-lighted cigar in his mouth, pausing only a moment to look in at the half-opened door of Mrs Chamberlain to say, "I'm going to the houses"'.[20] Having inspected his orchids, Chamberlain would then engage in political work in his library for the rest of the day. A speaking tube connected him to his secretary J. Wilson in the next room, and a telephone and the telegraph to the rest of his world. As he worked, he smoked cigars, and occasionally cigarettes, with hardly a break. Joe kept his cigarettes in an inscribed silver case, presented to him by a former Liberal colleague; the inscription read, 'To J.C., Xmas 1888. Let us smoke the pipe of peace. Yours W.V. Harcourt'. Chamberlain sat with his back to Gladstone - on the wall behind him as he worked at his desk was a photograph of the Liberal leader. It was to remain in its place after the rupture over Home Rule. Periodically, Chamberlain received deputations in his library - for example, Methodist ministers anxious about the residency requirements of the Reform Bill in January 1885, schoolmasters keen to secure his support for a pension scheme in October 1896 and grocers seeking changes to the Food and Drugs Bill in April 1899. Three men, leading a procession of more than 500 of the unemployed, received a less cordial reception in October 1885. Chamberlain - protected by policemen in the house - saw them, condemned their actions as 'ostentatious' and 'cruel' and refused to address a meeting at the town hall called on the subject of unemployment. 'The men', it was reported, 'marched into town, loudly expressing dissatisfaction'.[21]

It was on Sunday afternoons that the family came together. After lunch there would be a walk along the winding paths in the gardens and, on occasion, Chamberlain would row his daughters across the lake. 'Sometimes we went straight out, which was all right', Hilda was still grumbling years later, 'but sometimes he would begin by going down the houses and this was always much deplored as he would stay too long in the hothouses, talking to Cooper (or "Coops" as we called him) the gardener who had been with him at Southbourne'. When they were younger, Chamberlain went through the *Graphic* or the *Illustrated London News* with his

---

[20] University of Birmingham, Cadbury Research Library, BC5/10/6.
[21] *Edinburgh Evening News,* 21 October 1885; *Cork Examiner,* 31 October 1896; *Western Times,* 4 April 1899.

daughters on a Sunday afternoon. In later years they would join him in the conservatory to discuss the political situation. 'Looking back I can see how it was that all of us girls were anti-suffrage', Hilda wrote. 'Unlike so many women we never had a sense of inferiority ground into us. In the family Papa made no difference in his conversation between girls and boys and we were as likely to hear political secrets or ideas talked of when only we were present, as if Austen and Neville were there, too'. Her father, Hilda added, 'would always talk of all the political affairs before us, trusting absolutely to us not to talk unwisely to others ... (and) 'rous(e) every one of us to join in the talk and give of our best'. Only when the conversation turned to scientific matters would Joe have little to say, leaving Beatrice and Austen to do the talking.[22]

In the public mind Joe spent the greater part of his time at Highbury cultivating his orchids. Each morning when he stepped out of 40 Prince's Gardens, there were orchids in his lapel - usually odontoglossums - sent up by train, with other flowers for the house, from Highbury the evening before. Intent, as a young man, on getting to know the pot and kettle manufacturer Archibald Kenrick, Chamberlain discovered not only his daughter Harriet, whom he married in July 1861, but also the pleasures of growing orchids and other plants. Though he maintained a good garden and greenhouses from that time on, it was with his arrival at Highbury that his passion for horticulture became an integral part of his public image. At first, Chamberlain didn't always appear in public with orchids in his lapel - he was sporting violets when he resigned from office over Home Rule on 15 March 1886 - but they did increasingly become his emblem, 'very much more "his flower" than ... the primrose was Lord Beaconsfield's'. The orchids in his lapels - 'brilliant as ever this session', it was reported in early 1893 -

---

[22] University of Birmingham, Cadbury Research Library, BC5/10/5, BC/10/6. There is much detail about Chamberlain's relations with his children in Hilda's reminiscences – from his feigned disbelief at their excellent school reports to the 'hideous' black vase they clubbed together to buy him which he kept on his toilette 'for years and years after'. Robert Rhodes James, *The British Revolution: British Politics 1880-1939* (1978), p. 169 describes Highbury as being a place where 'Chamberlain dominated a ... subservient *menage* ... the women were there to ... applaud him' - which is wholly at odds with Hilda's account.

eclipsed the carnations grown, and worn each day, by his fellow parliamentarian Henry Broadhurst. Chamberlain chose special orchids for special occasions – for example, he chose a very beautiful white specimen with a gold centre to celebrate the capitulation of the Boers on 31 May 1902. The orchids could not be left behind when Joe visited South Africa in winter 1902-3: 300 of them were stored in the freezing room of the *Good Hope*.[23]

The orchid houses at Highbury, lit by electricity, were joined together, being reached by walking from the conservatory through 'a glass-covered, mosaic-floored, plant-furnished promenade'. There were nine orchid houses in 1888, but over the next decade another five were brought into use. In other glass houses plants of other kinds – begonias, cyclamens and chrysanthemums, amongst them – were also under cultivation. This was clearly a large-scale operation on which Chamberlain spent 'a modest fortune', new varieties of orchid being 'constantly purchased' – estimates of the value of the many thousands of orchid plants at Highbury were put at anywhere between £8,000 and £20,000. All of the orchids were assigned a number, enabling Chamberlain to record in a book a brief description of each plant, its country of origin and its place of purchase. This was his principal contribution to the cultivation of orchids at Highbury; he might have worn an apron and smoked a pipe when he entered his orchid houses, but he left the potting, re-potting and cross-fertilization of his orchids to three gardeners who did nothing else but look after these plants. 'So close is the attention Mr Chamberlain pays to his orchids that he is believed by his gardeners to know every plant', it was reported by a provincial newspaper; whilst his own local newspaper declared him to be 'probably now the largest private grower in England'. It was reported – inaccurately but very entertainingly – that during a visit to Paris Chamberlain had bought and destroyed a rare orchid; 'I have one of that kind', Joe is supposed to have said, 'and I would rather nobody else in Europe had another'. Certainly visitors to Highbury often left with a specimen they had admired, and these famous

---

[23] *Edinburgh Evening Express*, 7 January 1886, 4 December 1902; *Birmingham Daily Post*, 27 September 1889; *Aberdeen Evening Express*, 10 February 1893; *Evening Telegraph*, 5 December 1902. Whilst in Cape Colony the railway station at Kwefontein was re-named Highbury by Mary Chamberlain: *Sunderland Daily Echo*, 11 February 1903.

orchids unsurprisingly frequently won prizes – for example, in December 1899 a new plant produced by cross-fertilization was singled out for recognition by the Royal Horticultural Society. Joe's love of orchids was shared by Neville and his daughter Ida, whose drawings of specimens from the collection were proudly shown by her father to visitors along with the real things. The Highbury orchid collection, depleted after Neville had taken what he wanted, was sold for £826 in London in April 1915.[24]

IV

Highbury was surrounded by extensive gardens and a park. As the years passed Chamberlain added substantially to the twenty five acres he had originally bought. Eventually the gardens and park extended to one hundred acres. It was important in an age of encroaching house-building for a country seat to preserve its views. Intended to make clear Joe's importance to the politicians and journalists who visited, the gardens were truly magnificent, 'arguably the most elaborate of the many gardens created by Birmingham industrialists and professional men in the late nineteenth century and, due to Chamberlain's high political profile, widely written about'.[25] The gardens were the work of Edward Milner, assisted by his son John. Milner had begun his horticultural career under Joseph Paxton at Chatsworth and also created the pleasure gardens at Buxton and the gardens at Bodnant. Though Milner's plan had largely been carried out by the mid-1880s, new features continued to be added until Chamberlain was incapacitated. Chamberlain was intimately involved, choosing the plants – he had an especial liking

---

[24] *Derby Daily Telegraph,* 14 June 1884; *Evening Telegraph,* 3 February 1888, 5 December 1902; *Edinburgh Evening News,* 15 November 1888; *Birmingham Daily Post,* 27 September 1889; *York Herald,* 30 August 1893; *Coventry Evening Telegraph,* 30 March 1896; *Sheffield Evening Telegraph.* 6 December, 8 December 1899.

[25] P. Ballard, *Highbury Park, Moseley, Birmingham. Historic Landscape Appraisal* (Birmingham, 2009), p. 25. This is a very thorough discussion of the formation and decline of the gardens at Highbury. Ballard points out that unfortunately no notebooks or planting plans for the gardens have survived. Also see P. Ballard, '"Rus in Urbe": Joseph Chamberlain's Gardens at Highbury, Moor Green, Birmingham 1879-1914' in *Garden History,* vol. 14, no.1 (1986), pp. 61-76.

for rhododendrons – and supervising the designs, declaring that 'a straight line is always exceedingly ugly to look on'.[26]

There was something to admire in the gardens all through the year. There were hollies, which in winter 'flourish amazingly'. The first sight of the year were the 800 daffodils and 6,500 tulips planted in the Dutch garden, which was crossed by terracotta paths. Banks of rhododendrons 'in first rate condition' surrounded the house and grew alongside the carriage drive, flowering to glorious effect in May. There were also three large rose gardens – the favourite flower of Mary – a garden given over to irises, an Italian garden featuring a small pool and fountain, and a rock garden. Milner believed that a landscape was not complete without water, and created a lake, complete with islands, bridges and waterfalls, and two pools. Chamberlain would often sit by one of these pools and contemplate his political manoeuvres. Around the entrance lodge were magnolias and bamboos. Beyond the gardens lay the park where mature trees were deliberately left undisturbed.[27]

During the summer months Chamberlain opened his gardens to Liberal Unionist activists. 'The guests were chiefly of the working classes', it was reported of one such event, 'sturdy Unionists to a man'. Up to 1,500 people would be admitted to these garden parties, and permitted to inspect the conservatory, with its large palms, banana tree, fountain and gold fish pond, before settling down to listen to a speech from Joe and finishing off with singing and dancing. If it rained – and it often did – the event was moved into the hall, Joe not wishing to waste the speech he had written. Before his speech Chamberlain would move amongst the crowds. This was Joe at his amiable best. He would chat to men he barely knew, giving them the great pleasure of demonstrating their intimate acquaintance with the famous statesman to their wives and daughters. At one garden party, in August 1887, one young man, requesting Joe's orchid, 'received it with exultation and, carrying it

---

[26] Quoted in Ballard, *Highbury Park,* p. 37.
[27] University of Birmingham, Cadbury Research Library, JC 4/12; *Dover Express,* 28 December 1888; *Yorkshire Evening Post,* 28 March 1898; *Gardener's Magazine,* 18 April 1903; *Manchester Evening News,* 10 June 1907. Also see University of Birmingham, Cadbury Research Library, C/9/21-22 for albums containing photographs of the gardens at Highbury.

in triumph to a young lady who was sitting a few yards away, he fixed it to her breast'. The final garden party at Highbury took place in June 1914. The stricken Chamberlain was 'wheeled about in a bath chair on the terrace in front of the house and responded to the enthusiastic cheering of his supporters by raising his hat'.[28]

Needless to say, a small army of gardeners toiled away at Highbury. We know the stories of a few of these men. Edward Cooper had been with Chamberlain since 1880 and, at the time of his death, in 1892, was head gardener, living in a cottage in the grounds. A married man with a fondness for chrysanthemums, he died suddenly as the result of a brain haemorrhage. His wife had previously lost her voice, but the shock was said to have restored her powers of speech. John Deacon was head gardener at the time of his death in 1912 and in charge of the orchids. He had family worries, but, according to his wife, was 'quite cheerful when he left home' on the day he died. He drowned in one of the pools. He may have taken his own life, but a verdict of death by misadventure was recorded on account of the steep banks. Edward Andrews, at the time of his death in 1897, was 'a quiet, steady fellow' who been working at Highbury for fourteen years. Stricken with grief at the death of his mother, he hanged himself in a cow shed on Austen's farm.[29]

V

Everything changed at Highbury after the summer of 1906. There were no more speeches from the balcony above the great hall, no more political powwows in the library, far fewer dinner parties, only

---

[28] *Whitstable Times,* 27 August 1887; *Sheffield Daily Telegraph,* 30 August 1887; *Birmingham Daily Gazette,* 29 July, 12 August 1889; Glasgow *Herald,* 12 August 1889; *Worcestershire Chronicle,* 22 June 1895; *Belfast News Letter,* 26 May 1899; *Aberdeen Journal,* 2 June 1906; *Newcastle Journal,* 8 June 1914.

[29] *Gloucester Citizen,* 4 May 1892; *Tamworth Herald,* 7 May 1892; *Edinburgh Evening News,* 14 December 1897; *Exeter and Plymouth Gazette,* 15 December 1897; *Evening Telegraph,* 11 January 1912; *Manchester Courier,* 13 January 1912. For the farm at Highbury see M. Perrie. 'Hobby Farming among the Birmingham bourgeoisie: the Cadburys and the Chamberlains on their Suburban Estates c. 1880-1914', *Agricultural History Review,* vol. 61, no.1 (2013), pp. 111-34.

one more garden party. Chamberlain's stroke – which took place at Prince's Gardens on 11 July – left him paralyzed down the right side and unable to speak at all clearly nor intelligibly or to keep his monocle in his right eye. His doctors spoke of an eventual recovery, and so the family ascribed his unexpected withdrawal from public life to a severe attack of gout.[30] Reports, in August 1906, that Joe was so incapacitated that he was confined to his room were dismissed as 'incorrect'. It was two months before Chamberlain returned to Highbury, a broken ankle offered as the explanation for the wheelchair used to convey him from his train to his carriage. The telephone at Highbury, Austen complained after his father's return, 'is going constantly. It is an unmitigated nuisance, and the pressmen are hovering about the place all day.' Chamberlain was, of course, a celebrity, and the interest in what had happened to him was immense. His arrivals at, and departures from Highbury, over the next year were always reported in the press. These reports always sought to be encouraging. When Chamberlain left Highbury in February 1907 for three months in Cannes, it was announced that 'on his return he will be able to resume his political work'. When, the following July, he departed for Prince's Gardens, it was reported that he walked, with assistance from Mary, to the train, and, 'looking well and bright and a good healthy colour', 'nodded smilingly' at the people who raised their hats. In October 1908 Chamberlain was said to have spent long periods in his gardens and 'been able to take several long drives'. At Highbury Chamberlain continued to make his views on the issues of the day known to Austen, and to the wider world in letters to the newspapers. There were also visits from, amongst others, Balfour and the rising star of the Conservative Party, F.E. Smith. To the very end politics filled Joe's head.[31]

---

[30] University of Birmingham, Cadbury Research Library, BC5/10/6, for Hilda's recollection that her father, often afflicted with gout when he eased up, would observe that he 'had had gout in every capital in Europe'.

[31] *Evening Telegraph,* 17 August 1906, 28 September 1906, 25 July 1907; *Aberdeen Journal,* 18 August 1906, 15 June 1907, 22 September 1909, 30 September 1910; *Manchester Courier,* 4 February 1907, 5 July 1907; *Dundee Courier,* 2 March 1907; *Derby Daily Telegraph,* 29 September 1910.

VI

'Highbury is left to my brother, and is his now', Neville Chamberlain observed soon after his father's death. It was very much Joe's house. His body was returned to the house the night before his funeral on 6 July 1914. It was then a case of deciding what to do with Highbury. No member of the family wanted to live there. Not Austen, not Mary, who took up residence in Prince's Gardens. In April 1915 the furniture and effects were sold off. 'There was a good attendance, which included several Americans', it was reported. 'No big prices, however, were realised.' With his father's mansion empty, Austen made it available for use as a hospital for wounded soldiers. After the end of the war Austen presented the house to the Highbury Trustees – who also raised the funds to buy the land - and it continued to operate as a hospital, with the glasshouses serving as wards and an operating theatre. In June 1923 two patients suffering from tuberculosis were killed when a specially-constructed wooden ward in the grounds burnt down. In 1937 Highbury, with the glasshouses now demolished, was converted into a home for elderly women. Joe's library, housing items associated with his political career, became a small museum in his memory. So Chamberlain's mansion was put to good use after his death. But, for all these new uses, Highbury could never be for Birmingham anything other than Joe's very public private house.[32]

---

[32] *Liverpool Echo,* 15 September 1914, 5 August 1918; *Sunday Post,* 21 March 1915; *Sunday Mirror,* 26 March 1915; *Lichfield Mercury,* 2 April 1915; *Aberdeen Evening Express,* 29 April 1915; *Aberdeen Journal,* 15 June 1923.

Illustrations

1. Joseph Chamberlain, sporting his favourite orchid, the odontoglossum. A previous owner of the postcard, clearly an admirer of Joe, has appended the comment 'Just like him'.

2. Highbury at night. Doctored photographs of well-known buildings with their lights blazing were popular at the turn of the twentieth century – another widely-circulating postcard featured the Council House in Birmingham at night.

3. The entrance at Highbury.

4. South front of Highbury.

5. South front – another view.

6. The hall at Highbury, with a huge fern in the centre.

7. The hall – another view.

8. The hall – another view.

9. The library at Highbury – the room where Chamberlain worked.

10. The orchid houses at Highbury.

ILLUSTRATIONS

11. The interior of one of the orchid houses at Highbury.

12. Visitors to Highbury, Easter 1889:

At rear (left to right): Duke of St. Albans; Marquis of Hartington
At front (left to right): Lord Camperdown; Mary Chamberlain; Earl Selbourne; Duchess of St. Albans; Lady Palmer; Joseph Chamberlain.

Duke of St. Albans: William Anelius Aubery de Vere Beauclerk (1840-98) followed Chamberlain from the Liberals into the Liberal Unionists. Joe enjoyed his hospitality at his Gothic Nottinghamshire mansion, Bestwood. 'As an owner he seldom possessed an animal of much merit ...', it was reported after his death of this great enthusiast for horse racing. (*London Standard*, 11 May 1898).
Marquis of Hartington: Spencer Compton Cavendish (1833-1908) could be described as the last in a long line of Whig politicians. His initial hopes that Gladstone might withdraw from politics and the Liberals abandon Irish Home Rule were not realised. He and the much more charismatic Chamberlain became uneasy allies in leading Liberal Unionism.
Lord Camperdown: Robert Adam Haldane Duncan (1841-1918) was a great champion of Scotland in the House of Lords and, after 1886, a leader of the Liberal Unionist cause in that country. He was a J.P. in Warwickshire, where he owned extensive estates.
Earl Selbourne: Roundell Palmer (1812-95) won numerous prizes at Oxford and, after being called to the Bar, served as a Liberal MP at various times between 1847 and 1872. When he broke with Gladstone over Irish Home Rule, it was not the first time the two men had failed to see eye-to-eye.
Duchess of St. Albans: Grace Bernal-Osborne (d. 1926) was the second wife of the Duke of Albans, and the daughter of the Liberal MP Ralph Bernal Osborne, who was so injudicious in his comments that 'the wonder is that the fellow was never pitched in a horse pond, as he richly deserved'. (*Derby Daily Telegraph*, 25 November 1926).
Lady Palmer: Sophia Palmer (1852-1915) was the daughter of the 1st Earl of Selbourne. She married Charles Fraquet, Comte de Franqueville in 1903, who, after her death, asked his sister-in-law to write a biography of her (1919).

ILLUSTRATIONS

DISTINGUISHED VISITORS AT HIGHBURY.

LORD CANTERDOWN. DUKE OF ST. ALBANS. MARQUIS OF HASTINGS. THE RIGHT HON. JOS. CHAMBERLAIN, M.P.
MRS. JOS. CHAMBERLAIN. EARL SPENCER. DUCHESS OF ST. ALBANS.

BIRMINGHAM FACES AND PLACES.

13. The men who came to dinner: Jesse Collings (1831-1920), Liberal Unionist MP for Bordesley after 1886 and Chamberlain's most trusted political henchman.

14. The men who came to dinner: J.T. Bunce (1828-99), editor of the *Birmingham Daily Post* and, in this key position, played a vital role in bolstering local support for Joe.

15. The men who came to dinner: R.W. Dale (1829-95), Congregationalist minister from Carr's Lane, who provided the moral underpinning to Chamberlain's political work.

ILLUSTRATIONS

16. Highbury today.

17 Highbury today.

Highbury today.

About the Author

Stephen Roberts is currently writing about the MPs who represented Bedford between 1832 and 1868 for the History of Parliament. He is the author or editor of ten books on Chartism and four books on Victorian Birmingham. He was for many years a Fellow in the University of Birmingham.

THE BIRMINGHAM BIOGRAPHIES SERIES

Already published:

Dr J.A. Langford 1823-1903: A Self-Taught Working Man and the Sale of American Degrees in Victorian Britain. 65 pp, 8 photographs, 2014. ISBN: 978 1495475122. £5.99.

Sir Benjamin Stone 1838-1914: Photographer, Traveller and Politician. 102 pp, 20 photographs, 2014. ISBN: 978 1499265521. £7.99.

Mocking Men of Power: Comic Art in Birmingham 1861-1914. 60 cartoons, 2014. ISBN: 978 1502764560. £8.99. (with Roger Ward)

Sir Richard Tangye 1833-1906: A Cornish Entrepreneur in Victorian Birmingham. 65 pp, 2015. ISBN: 978-1512207910. £4.99

These books can be ordered from Amazon and other booksellers.

Forthcoming

To The Editor: A Selection of Letters from the Newspapers of Victorian Birmingham

Printed in Great Britain
by Amazon